Contents

C000142163

FRIENDS OF THE CROMFORD CANAL

Patron: Julian Richards   President: Brian Blessed

The Friends of the Cromford Canal is an organisation whose aim is
to promote the restoration to navigation of the Cromford Canal,
its connection to the national waterways system, and the conservation, use,
maintenance and development of all its features, for the public benefit.

Chairman: Patrick Morriss 07989 282291
Membership Secretary: Yvonne Shattower 0115 946 4479

Visit www.cromfordcanal.org.uk
for more information including both historic and present day photographs,
membership form and sales items.

FRONT COVER: Langley Bridge Lock No.14 on the fortieth anniversary of its re-opening by volunteers of the Erewash Canal Preservation & Development Association.   Photo: Mike Harrison

BACK COVER: The horse boat approaching Lawn Bridge on its way to Cromford during the World Heritage Site Discovery Days weekend in late October.   Photo: Hugh Potter

Published 2010 by the Friends of the Cromford Canal
© Written and compiled by Michael Harrison & Valerie Roberts
Maps: Hugh Potter
All uncredited photographs by the authors
ISBN 978-0-9544482-1-9

All proceeds from the sale of this booklet will be used to further the aims of
The Friends of the Cromford Canal

Foreword

by Patrick Morriss, Chairman
Friends of the Cromford Canal

Soon after the formation of the Friends of the Cromford Canal in 2002, it was decided that one of the first tasks was to produce a Walker's Guide to the Cromford Canal. It has since proved to be our most popular publication, assisting both locals and visitors from afar to explore this popular waterway and at the same time raising funds for the ongoing restoration efforts. I would like to welcome you to this second edition of the Walker's Guide. The route of the waterway is rich in history and crosses some of the most beautiful countryside in the Midlands. This book will guide you along the canal, while at the same time indicating the sights of this historic area with all its natural attractions.

The main line of the canal can be divided into three sections. Each section is detailed within this booklet and can be taken as a separate walk. The fit walkers amongst you may want to complete the whole 15 miles in one. For the rest, each section is covered as an individual walk of between four and six miles.

The first walk is the southern section and goes from Langley Mill to Ironville and crosses open meadows and the nature reserves of the Brinsley Flash wetlands. We then gradually climb the unfortunately now derelict flight of seven locks, up to the junction with the Pinxton Arm which is described separately. Just beyond the junction is the Codnor Park Reservoir, an attractive area of open water and full of wildlife.

The second walk is the central section and covers an amazing variety of countryside. Starting in Golden Valley, we then follow the course of the Butterley Tunnel overland. This is one of the longest canal tunnels in the country. The canal walk then passes through Lower Hartshay to Sawmills, where it becomes elevated above the rooftops of the local houses.

The third, northern section is the best known part of the canal. At the start of this walk an unfortunate detour, giving views over the Amber Valley, is required to by-pass two industrial sites that were built on the line of the canal in the 1960s. Once this is behind you, the Derwent Valley is reached and is followed all the way to the end of the canal at Cromford Wharf. There are good views across the valley and areas are seen that were in the forefront of the Industrial Revolution. This section is within the Derwent Valley Mills World Heritage site, the only WHS in the East Midlands and is the longest length of canal in a WHS in England.

**Enjoy your walks and at the same time help us to restore the
Cromford Canal for future generations.**

Cromford Canal Walk: Stage 1
Langley Mill to Codnor Park - 4 miles

The Cromford Canal joined the Erewash Canal at this point, where the latter swung left and terminated in twin basins by the main road

The Cromford Canal begins at Langley Mill where it joins the Erewash Canal below the A608 Bridge No. 49. *(The bridge numbers used throughout this guide are the official Cromford Canal bridge numbers. These should not be confused with the modern number plates using a different system, recently fitted to some of the bridges by British Waterways.)*

Langley Bridge Lock No. 14, the only operable one on the canal, is immediately above the bridge. This lock was restored from a derelict condition by volunteer members of the Erewash Canal Preservation & Development Association and re-opened to navigation in May 1973.

Just above this lock, the derelict Nottingham Canal makes a junction with the Cromford. The swing bridge and stop lock at the entrance to this canal, giving access to the Great Northern Basin, were restored at the same time as Langley Bridge Lock. The Great Northern Inn adjoins the basin. Note also the former Nottingham Canal toll house, restored in 2008 by the ECP&DA, just beyond the swing bridge.

Langley Mill Boatyard's dry dock, workshop and moorings now occupy the first length of the Cromford Canal above the junction. The towpath was originally on the west side of the canal along this next section, but the public right of way was diverted when the area was opencast mined. The path therefore terminates at the boatyard boundary. Beyond the boatyard the A610 bypass road crosses the canal line shortly above the site of Strutt's Lock No. 13. There is no public access through the boatyard so to start this walk we must, for the time being, make a diversion as follows. See the red dotted line on the map overleaf.

The derelict Nottingham Canal joins the Cromford Canal above Langley Bridge Lock No. 14. Note the restored toll office on the left.

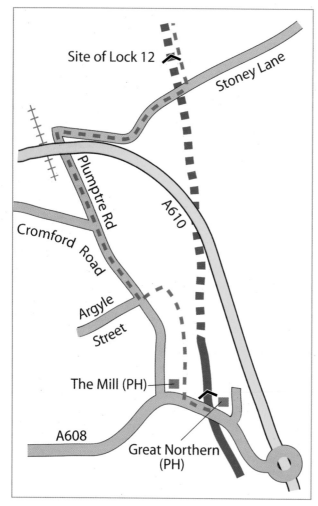

From the lock, turn right and walk along the main road towards Langley Mill passing the Esso station, over the River Erewash bridge and immediately turn right along a signed footpath between the river and what was formerly The Mill public house which stands on the corner of Cromford Road. Following the course of the river, we shortly pass behind Smith's flour mill. The remains of the former intake from the river to the water mill, which originally occupied this site, can be seen. The intake is well above the present river level which was lowered to reduce the risk of flooding in Langley Mill. Continue to follow the path adjacent to the left side of the river. (Do not cross the footbridge). Pass a weir on the river and then follow the path which turns left round the corner of an asbestos building and continue to meet Cromford Road, opposite Argyle Street.

Turn right along Cromford Road and continue past the Durham Ox public house (now closed). As Cromford Road bends to the left, keep straight on along Plumptre Road, and at the end, take the track straight ahead to the left of Plumptre Farmhouse.

Pass under the A610 bypass bridge (the railway is on your left) and follow the track round to the right (NOT the footpath straight ahead). Continue along this track, which is Stoney Lane, for some 400 yards and re-cross the River Erewash on a low level bridge. After a further 150 yards is the site of Stoney Lane Bridge No. 45 over the canal line and, just beyond, a public footpath to Brinsley Hill and Jacksdale is signed to the left.

Turn left along this signed footpath which is to the right of the actual canal line, but follows it closely. In a small copse on the left of the path is the site of Vickers Lock No. 12. This is not readily accessible, but the determined walker can scramble into the undergrowth where traces of the lock chamber coping stones can be found. Further to the left, the flashes on the River Erewash caused by mining subsidence can be seen.

Pass over a stile straight ahead into a second field and follow the path, then over another stile and small footbridge over a brook into a third field, and continue straight ahead with the hedge on your right. You are now on the canal line. After some 250 yards fork left at a stile (do not pass over this one) and continue, to cross a steel footbridge over the river. This is the site

The footbridge which replaces the former aqueduct over the River Erewash

of the aqueduct which carried the Cromford Canal over the River Erewash. When the river level is low, some remains of the brickwork of the aqueduct can be seen in the river on each side of the footbridge.

Follow the footpath straight across the field ahead, then over a double stile into the next one. There are no traces of the two Stoneyford Locks, Nos. 11 & 10, which were in this length. Continue over another double stile and across a third field to pass close to the right of what are now boarding kennels. This is the site of Boat Lane Bridge No. 41, which was immediately adjacent to a small old cottage which has now been replaced by a larger, rather attractive newly built stone and brick house on the same site.

Walkers queue to pass the stile into the Derbyshire Wildlife Trust section

Those wanting refreshment at this stage can visit Stoneyford Lodge, formerly the Boat Inn, which is up the track to the left beyond the railway bridge.

Carry straight on, with the modern kennels on your left, over another stile and into the section of the canal line now owned by the Derbyshire Wildlife Trust, see the adjacent interpretation board. Some remains of canalside stone wall are visible along the line of the fence on the left. Stoneyford Top Lock No. 9 was just above here, but again there is no trace nowadays. This whole area has not only suffered from deep mine subsidence, but the entire landscape has been altered by opencast coal workings. Brinsley Flash is on the right.

Pass another stile, noting yellow direction arrows and continue along the path to the right of the fence. We are still on the canal line here. The next stile is by the site of Slaley's Bridge No. 40. Another footpath goes off to the left, but we carry straight on.

Butterley Company Lock No. 8 was in this next section. This length can become very muddy in wet weather, and some sections are crossed on wooden boardwalks. Shortly after passing a second interpretation board about the Erewash Meadows Nature Reserve, we come to the remains of a railway bridge.

Just here, pass over a stile and cross to the right over some running water via a small footbridge and continue ahead along the towpath. There are also walks from here along the railway embankment for those interested. The reed-filled canal bed, with a good towpath on the right, is now easily followed. This is the first length of obvious canal since leaving Langley Mill. Continuing along this towpath, we pass a wide section of the canal and further on a concrete weir across the channel now retains the water at a higher level. This was installed by the Butterley Company to maintain the water level for Codnor Park Forge after the canal was closed.

We shortly pass over the junction bridge which marks the entrance to the former Portland Basin on the right. This was a short branch of the canal which immediately crossed an aqueduct over the River Erewash and led to Jacksdale Wharf. Here was an interchange basin between the canal and the Mansfield & Pinxton Railway.

After passing over this bridge, keep to the left on the towpath and immediately pass the abutments of what had been a "Butterley Standard" steel bridge over the canal. Beyond here, there are a few remaining signs of the Codnor Park Forge buildings adjoining the canal on the left bank.

Marshall's Lock No. 6 with the former dry dock alongside

We now reach Bottom of Flight Lock No. 7, the first of the Codnor Park flight. Continue up to Marshall's Lock No. 6, where the remains of a narrow dry dock can be

These ruined buildings on the right now mark the site of the former canal maintenance yard and stables

seen alongside the lock chamber. This is the site of several working parties where the Friends of the Cromford Canal have been assisting Derbyshire Wildlife Trust in clearing the trees and undergrowth from around the lock chamber and the dock.

Above here on the towpath side are the former canal maintenance yard, cottage and stables. These buildings were intact until a few years ago, but they have now fallen into dereliction.

This is shortly followed by Gas House Lock No. 5. Although all of these locks are overgrown and partially filled with rubbish, the stone lock chambers are mostly intact and are still in a reasonable condition, but the lock gates have long since rotted away. Locks 7, 6 & 5 are grade 2 listed structures belonging to Derbyshire Wildlife Trust.

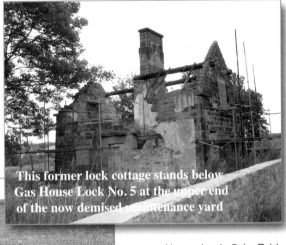

This former lock cottage stands below Gas House Lock No. 5 at the upper end of the now demised maintenance yard

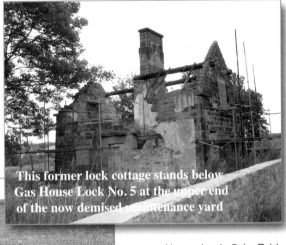

Railway Bridge No. 38 carries the main Erewash Valley line

Above Lock 5 is Bridge No. 38 carrying the main Erewash Valley railway line which marks the boundary between DWT and British Waterways property. The canal passes through the centre of the three arches and shortly reaches Smith's Lock No. 4.

Here can be seen the remains of the anchor bracket which held the bottom lock gate into its pivot point in the quoin stone. Note also, in the bottom gate recess, a deep groove caused by the ropes from the thousands of horse drawn boats which have passed this way. It is difficult to imagine now the large volume of traffic which formerly used this waterway.

Continue up into Ironville, a canalside village built by the Butterley Company for its workers. Adjacent to the towpath there are stone buildings, formerly canal stables, now used by a road transport firm. On the opposite side of the canal is another impressive stone building. This was formerly the Butterley Company Mechanics Institute, later the Butterley Colliery offices, now converted into attractive apartments.

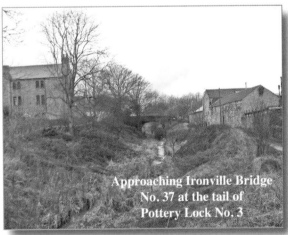

Approaching Ironville Bridge No. 37 at the tail of Pottery Lock No. 3

Pottery Lock No. 3

This is followed by Ironville Bridge No. 37, a fine stone arch bridge at the tail of Pottery Lock No. 3. This is the first surviving original bridge since we started our walk. Along the following short pound, on the left, there is a single storey stone building which was formerly a pottery, close by the water's edge. Note the doorway used for loading boats. Alongside the towpath opposite here is an interesting wall built using blocks of furnace slag.

This short pound leads to a second stone arch bridge (No. 36) below Boat Dock Lock No. 2. Note the iron guards on the bridge abutments. These were to protect the stonework from the wear caused by the towlines from the horse drawn boats, very necessary looking at the grooves worn in them. Alongside Lock 2 are the remains of a boat dock which was accessed by a channel from above the top lock.

The former pottery above Lock No. 3

Above this lock the canal channel has been deepened. There is now no sign of the Top Lock No. 1, which was obliterated and the site excavated in the 1980s. This was deemed necessary at the time to provide a flood relief channel for Codnor Park Reservoir which is just ahead. The level of the reservoir was also lowered and the large overflow weir constructed at the same time.

Here also is the junction with the Pinxton Branch which leaves to the right. The walk along this branch is well worth exploring and is described later in this guide. The bridge at the entrance carrying the main line towpath is another original intact stone arch bridge.

Codnor Park Reservoir and footbridge over the relief channel leading to the car park

Pass by this bridge and continue across the footbridge over the reservoir overflow to a small car park on the infilled canal line. This car park is convenient for those arranging return transport.

A catering van provides excellent hot food and drinks here, as well as limited toilet facilities. It is normally open from 8am to 1pm from Wednesday to Sunday.

Cromford Canal Walk: Stage 2
Codnor Park to Bullbridge - 5 miles

Starting from the car park on the canal line at the eastern end of Codnor Park Reservoir, the towpath passes between the reservoir on the right and the infilled canal on the left. Follow the path to the far end of the reservoir, through a another small car park now disused, cross the footbridge over the head of the reservoir then keep left to continue on the towpath towards Golden Valley. There is now some water in the canal to the left of the towpath which is nicely surfaced and now part of a green route from Ironville to Golden Valley. On the right is a path giving access to the hamlet of Golden Valley. Continuing

The infilled Golden Valley Bridge No. 34 is lost in the bushes to the left

ahead on the towpath, note the concrete milepost showing $10^1/2$ miles to Cromford. Carry on under the derelict steel Footbridge No. 35, passing a second access to Golden Valley, and along the cutting to the site of Golden Valley Bridge No. 34. Just before this bridge is a modern steel gate and a large stone building on the right believed to be a former Co-op which once received goods by canal. The bridge is now infilled and culverted so we must walk up a steep slope and turn to the right for a short distance, before crossing the road to the Newlands Inn car park. The inn is unfortunately closed.

Take care when crossing the road

Turn left to pass across the front of the pub, and then turn right over a stile to

Butterley Tunnel East Portal

rejoin the towpath, which continues in the deepening cutting to the eastern portal of Butterley Tunnel. This section is invariably very muddy. A water feeder from the drained Butterley Park Reservoir runs into the canal down concrete steps to the right of the portal. Retrace your route a short way and turn left up the stepped path to the narrow gauge Newlands Inn station of the Golden Valley Light Railway. See page 34 for details of the Midland Railway Centre. Alternatively, the station can be reached directly from the road by walking round the back of the Newlands Inn from the car park.

Over Butterley Tunnel

Having looked at the eastern portal of Butterley Tunnel and the narrow gauge railway station behind the Newlands Inn, retrace your steps to the road. Turn right and pass over the canal line at the site of Golden Valley Bridge No. 34, then take the first turn right onto Coach Road. This is a former toll road which ran through the Butterley Estate and closely follows the line of the tunnel. The road is still private and vehicular use is restricted, but the public footpath remains.

Walk straight up the road passing Golden Valley Caravan and Camping Park on the left. Continue ahead passing a right turn to the Midland Railway Centre and several "Private Road" signs and on to the old toll bar. There is a gate across at this point, beside a terrace of cottages and a farm. Pass over the stile to the left of the gate, and continue along the road.

Cottages by the old Toll Bar on Coach Road

Attractive former Butterley Estate houses by the entrance road to Butterley Hall, now the police headquarters

Note on the left here, the first of the ventilation shafts for the tunnel in the field just beyond the farm. This is a brick chimney-like structure in the centre of a mound of earth, which was made from the spoil drawn up the shaft when the tunnel was being constructed. The mound is still clearly apparent today, although long since grassed over. Pass by Butterley Park House on the left and a little further on is another vent on the right hand side, although this one is nowadays a rectangular concrete structure. Continuing along the road, there is a bridge over a derelict railway and after this a turn to the right, which leads to the Derbyshire Police helicopter unit and vehicle workshops. Again carry straight on, passing a turn to the left with an attractive former Butterley Estate Lodge House on the corner. In a short distance the headquarters of Derbyshire Constabulary at Butterley Hall is seen on the left, so please be on your best behaviour! On the right opposite this is a third tunnel vent standing on another mound covered in trees. This one is brick built and still retains the hemispherical iron grille on the top.

Butterley Tunnel ventilation shaft

On the road past here is an elaborate two-lane traffic control arrangement. Authorised vehicles must use a swipe card to lower the barriers, but pedestrians can pass unrestricted.

Follow the road then round to the right, past another entrance to the police headquarters and the former entrance to Butterley Engineering. This company has closed down and the site is being developed for housing. The road has now re-crossed the line of the tunnel which passes directly under the former Butterley

Traffic Control on
Butterley Coach Road

works. No doubt some walkers will be intrigued by the tunnel itself, which is unique in that it includes an underground loading wharf, which was accessed via a vertical shaft from the Butterley works. This is described in *Portal to Portal* by Des Greenwood. See page 35.

Continue down the road with new housing on the left, including Falkirk Avenue. This was named after the Falkirk Wheel, the well known Scottish boat lift, which was one of Butterley's

Hammersmith Station

best known, but sadly last, projects. We then reach the Ripley to Alfreton road, adjacent to the site of the now demised Butterley Company's main entrance.

Butterley reservoir, which supplied the canal, is immediately opposite. Cross the main road and turn left. Just before the sharp bend in the road, known locally as Butterley Corner, turn right down a track passing to the left of Lakeside Motors, and follow this track along the south side of the reservoir, passing Hammersmith

Meadows Nature reserve on the left. Shortly turn right on to a signed footpath alongside the far end of the reservoir. There is a British Waterways notice here, welcoming all to Butterley Reservoir.

Continue to the end of this path, turn left down a few steps and cross a small concrete bridge over the reservoir overflow. Pass through a works car park and over a stile in the far left hand corner which gives access to Hammersmith Station. This is the western terminus of the preserved railway operated by the Midland Railway Centre. Cross straight over the track via the boardwalk at the end of the platform. See also page 34.

Watching the trains

Photo: John Eggleshaw

Beware of occasional trains

Butterley Tunnel West Portal

Pass over another stile and turn left along a footpath behind the station platform. This path joins a track which continues to the road at the bottom of the hamlet of Hammersmith. Cross the road and turn right under the adjacent A38 bridge. Immediately through the bridge, turn left and over a stile to follow a signed public footpath, which passes to the left of Geeson's scrapyard. Continue down this often muddy path to reach the western portal of Butterley Tunnel. If you wish to inspect the portal more closely there is a flight of steps on the left leading down to it. Otherwise continue ahead taking the left fork of the path to re-join the towpath. Look back from here to see the western portal of the tunnel. The actual portal is hidden by a modern culvert which was installed to lengthen the tunnel when the A38 was built over this end.

Follow the overgrown and rather muddy towpath through the cutting, further on traversing a boardwalk and one-time landslip, then passing under a high level pipe bridge and continue ahead to the A610 embankment where the canal is culverted. Pass up a few steps, then up a long flight of steps to the A610 trunk road. Turn right for 40 yards along the pavement to a step, then stride over the crash barrier and cross the road.

Beware of fast moving traffic!

Stride over another crash barrier and pass down a similar staircase on the other side and over a stile to rejoin the towpath. We shortly pass the modernised former wharf house which stood at the end of Lower Hartshay Wharf. This was a short arm of the canal which has now disappeared. On then to the relatively modern Ripley Road Bridge No. 32 and pass under on the towpath. The Gate Inn, which is adjacent to this bridge, is currently closed. Follow what is now a good towpath with a concrete edge until just before Lower Hartshay village. On the left here is a long-abandoned riveted iron narrow boat, the remains

Terrace at Lower Hartshay, then.........and now

FCC Archive

of which are almost completely overgrown. The apparent channel finishes here at a fence across the canal with a stile for the towpath, beyond which the canal is infilled and grassed over. Pass through this short length which is used for grazing horses. On the left is an attractive terrace of old canalside houses.

After a second stile we come to Bridle Lane and the site of Hartshay Bridge No. 31, now destroyed. Note the green pipe which is still arched where it crossed the canal alongside the bridge.

Cross the lane and carry on along the signed footpath in front of the cottages on the right, by the infilled bed. Pass over a stile and follow the footpath directly across two fields with no sign of the canal, passing a second and then a third stile with a small footbridge

Looking back along the canal bed just through Hartshay Bridge No. 31. Note the green pipe

over a brook. Part way across the third field, turn left at the hedge to follow the signed footpath, keeping the hedge on your right. Pass over a stile close to the hedge to join the towpath and visible water channel just before Stavern's or Starvehimvalley Bridge No. 29, which is an intact original stone arch bridge.

Beyond this bridge, the channel has been widened to form a fishing lake, with the towpath on the right. Then the canal is again infilled and the path crosses the line to the left bank and joins a track, which continues on the left of the canal line to a fence with gate and stile. Pass over the stile and through the rear car park of The Excavator public house. Food is available here.

Continue through this car park to pass under Railway

The canal line under Railway Bridge No 28 passes through the car park of the Excavator Inn

Bridge No. 28, then round to the left and carry on through the front car park. This is on the line of the canal. Just beyond the car park is the short Buckland Hollow tunnel which is cut through solid rock. The canal channel through the tunnel is infilled, but one can walk through on the towpath.

Buckland Hollow Tunnel

The path now continues on the infilled canal bed for some way and then on the towpath to the right of the channel. There is a stone wall between the towpath and the A610 through Sawmills which is on a much lower level than the canal at this point. There are then several allotments with various greenhouses and sheds etc. on the canal line, but the public footpath is intact.

Gardens extended over the canal bed at Sawmills

Just after this, a section of the embankment has been removed where Lockwood's entrance road cuts across the line of the canal at main road level. Pass down the steps, across Lockwood's road and straight on up the track opposite and under the right hand arch of the stone

This entrance to Lockwood's works cuts through the canal embankment

Sawmills Bridge No. 26, to rejoin the canal.

Those interested in the history of the canal might want to first cross over this four-arched bridge to see one of the canal's hidden secrets. Directly across the entrance road to Lockwood's is the surviving western portal of the original canal bridge at this site. When the railway (now closed) was

built in 1875, its route would have crossed the canal twice on the level, so rather than build two opening bridges, the canal was diverted to stay on the north side of the railway.

Resuming our walk, beyond Sawmills Bridge No. 26 the channel is very overgrown but the towpath is still easily followed. After some 200 yards are the remains of

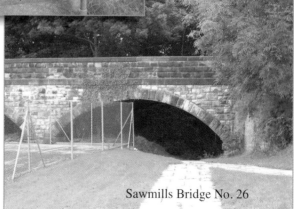

Sawmills Bridge No. 26

14

a gauging narrows in the canal. This is a stone built narrow section where the boats were gauged to determine the weight of their cargo. To the right of the towpath here behind a stone wall is a modern bungalow. This is adjacent to the site of the toll collector's stone cottage, long since demolished, but the original stone gate posts and the garden wall survive. Immediately beyond here is another concrete milepost, showing 6 miles to Cromford.

Continue until a signed junction is reached indicating a turn to the right opposite a greenhouse, just before a stone cottage. Turn right here, down the steps to emerge from behind St Mary's Mission Church on to the A610. This is the site of Bullbridge Aqueduct, a section of which over the road and railway was demolished in

St Mary's Mission in Sawmills adjacent to the site of Bullbridge Aqueduct

1968. Cross directly over the road and straight ahead to the railway line. Climb over the stile and cross the railway via the boardwalk. A footbridge has been proposed here, but in the meantime, **please take care as trains pass here at 100mph!**

Over the stile beyond the railway, take the left hand fork of the path and up the steps to return to canal level. Continue to a wall of stone blocks across the canal. Although you will not realise it, you have crossed the aqueduct over the River Amber. Follow the path to the left alongside a stone house which has been built on the canal line. Look over the wall to your left to see Drover's Way passing under the canal far below. This part of the aqueduct is still intact. The path now passes to the left of a bungalow which has also been built on the canal line.

Bull Bridge No. 19 and Bullbridge Cottages

After this a short section of the canal is in water, with the towpath on the left as far as Bull Bridge No. 19. This bridge is intact although filled in. The nearby Canal Inn here also serves food.

This is the end of the second section of the walk.

15

The Leawood
Pump in Steam

Photo: Hugh Potter

The Leawood Pump

The Cromford Canal Company was formed by Act of Parliament in 1789, and the canal was completed and opened to traffic in 1794. It operated successfully until 1844, which was a particularly dry year and the canal suffered badly from lack of water. This was overcome temporarily by hiring a pump to supplement the water supply by raising water from the nearby River Derwent. In 1845 the Canal Company decided on a permanent solution to this problem, and ordered a new pump. The pump we see today was eventually installed in 1849, at a cost of £2,900, after some negotiations with the Manchester, Matlock and Midland Joint Railway Company, who were at that time in the process of building the new line to Manchester, the temporary pump being on the line of the new track. The Midland Railway, as the MMMJR later became, subsequently purchased the canal.

Photo: Mike Kelley

Stoking one of the two boilers

Perhaps the most well known feature of the Cromford Canal is the engine house and accompanying boiler house. Standing between the canal and the river, adjacent to Wigwell Aqueduct, the stonework is of a very high standard and looks in as good a condition today as it did over 150 years ago. The engine was built by Graham and Company of Milton Ironworks, Elsecar. It is supplied with steam at 40psi by 2 locomotive-type boilers, built by Hawthorne Leslie and Co. from Tyneside for the Midland Railway Company in 1900. The steam passes to a 50 inch diameter steam cylinder, the piston of which has a 9 foot stroke. This is connected, via the massive beam which is 33 feet long and weighs 27 tons, to the pump plunger. This is capable of pumping 4 tons of water per stroke and 7 strokes per minute, a total of over 40,000 tons of water per 24 hours. The reason for this apparent over capacity was that the Canal Company was only allowed to pump water from the river from 8.00pm on Saturdays to 8.00pm on Sundays. This was to ensure that the river flow was not depleted for driving the many water mills in the valley at that time. The long summit pound of the canal from Codnor Park to Cromford therefore had to act as a reservoir to enable traffic to keep going all week. At that time, traffic volume was considerable - 300,000 tons in 1849.

To obtain further details and information on the engine, a visit to the pump house is highly recommended, especially on one of the weekends when the engine is in steam. Although owned by Derbyshire County Council, Leawood Pumphouse is restored, maintained and operated by a group of volunteers, who also look after the Middleton Top Engine on the Cromford and High Peak Railway. More volunteers are always welcomed.

Contact: The Leawood Pump House, C/o Countryside Service,
Middleton Top Visitor Centre, Derbyshire. Tel: 01629 823204

CROMFORD

Gregory Tunnel
East Portal

Cromford Wharf
Lawn Bridge
River Derwent
1
2
Leawood Pump
Nightingale Arm
Railway End Bridge
or Browns Bridge
7   8
Gregory Tunnel
Lea Shaw Bridge
9
12 Sims Bridge
13 Whatstandwell Bridge
13A Crich Council Footbridge

Fishermans Path Bridge 3
Lea Wood Aqueduct 4
Cattle Creep Bridge 5
Swing Bridge (Towpath) 6
High Peak Aqueduct 7

WHATSTANDWELL

Chase Bridge
14

AMBERGATE
19
18
15
16 16 17
Grattons Bridge
Poysers Bridge
Lime Works Bridge
Hag
Tunnel
26
27

Bull Bridge 19
Towing Path Swing B
Bull Bridge 21
River Amber Bridge 2
Railway Bridge 23
Culvert Bridge 24
Bridge 25

Saw Mills Bridge
or Brick Yard Br

Railway Bridge
Starvehimvalley or Starvern Bridge
Malthouse

River Derwent

The Feeder to the Canal
at Cromford

CROMFORD
2½
MILES

One of only
3 remaining
original mileposts

THE CROMFORD CANAL

18

Pinxton Wharf
looking towards
the end

Canal in water
Canal bed intact
Canal bed destroyed

Top Lock Bridge 1
Butterley Co Bridge 2
Ironville Bridge 3
Railway Bridge 4
Fletchers Row Bridge 5
Oakes Tramway Bridge 6
Red Bridge 7

PINXTON

Palmerston Swing Bridge
LNER Bridge ⑬
Colliery Office Bridge ⑫
⑪

Cutts Bridge ⑩
Pinxton Arm ⑨
⑧ Railway Bridge

Pye Bridge

⑦
⑤ ⑥

IRONVILLE
④ CODNOR PARK LOCKS 1–7

Butterley Reservoir

nber

Butterley Park   Codnor
Reservoir   Park
③③   Reservoir

low Tunnel

SHAY ㉛②

Ripley Road Bridge   Butterley Tunnel

artshay Bridge

Golden Valley Bridge   ③④ ③⑤   Butterley Co Bridge

Portland Basin
㊳ River Erewash
LNER Bridge

③⑨
BUTTERLEY CO LOCK 8   Slaleys Bridge
④⓪
STONEYFORD LOCK 9
Stoneyford Lane Bridge ④①

STONEYFORD DEEP LOCK 10
STONEYFORD SHALLOW LOCK 11
Bentley Bridge ④②
Erewash Aqueduct ④④
VICKER'S LOCK 12
Stoney Lane Bridge ④⑤

TOP OF FLIGHT LOCK 1
BOAT DOCK LOCK 2
Lock No 2 Bridge 36
POTTERY LOCK 3
Ironville Bridge 37
SMITH'S LOCK 4
Railway Bridge 38
GAS HOUSE LOCK 5
MARSHALLS LOCK 6
BOTTOM OF FLIGHT LOCK 7

STRUTT'S LOCK 13 ④⑥
Marshalls Bridge ④⑦
Beggarlea Bridge

LANGLEY BRIDGE LOCK 14
Nottingham Road Bridge ④⑨

LANGLEY MILL

Distance plaque by
Lock No 14
at Langley Mill

19

Cromford Canal Walk: Stage 3
Bullbridge to Cromford Wharf - 6 miles

Bullbridge Cottages

This section begins from the towpath just before Bull Bridge No. 19. Immediately by the bridge are Bullbridge Cottages on the right, with what were probably former Canal Company stables underneath. The bridge is intact but infilled and we must pass up from the towpath and across the road. The Canal Inn, which serves food, is nearby.

At Bullbridge, a major diversion is necessary to detour around land sold off by British Waterways in the mid-1960s. From Bull Bridge No. 19 to Hag Tunnel, the canal was purchased by Stevenson's dye works who built a road along the canal line. Following the closure of the works in 2008, the site is scheduled for redevelopment.

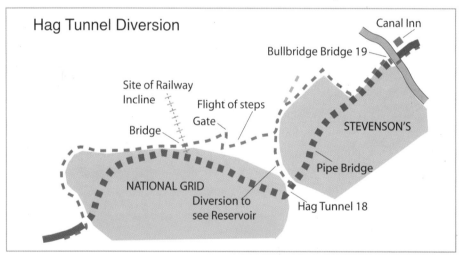

Hag Tunnel Diversion

Canal Inn

Bullbridge Bridge 19

STEVENSON'S

Site of Railway Incline

Flight of steps

Gate

Bridge

Pipe Bridge

NATIONAL GRID

Diversion to see Reservoir

Hag Tunnel 18

Carefully cross the road to take the signed footpath between the former canalside building and the bridge parapet. Look straight ahead along the line of the canal to a distant metal bridge with a sign on it saying "Caution! 10ft 6in Clearance". This is in its original position and crosses the now infilled canal line. It carries water mains from the Derwent Valley reservoirs towards Nottingham and was built with plenty of headroom for canal boats! The path follows the right hand side of the canal line, along

Black pipe bridge indicates canal line through Stevenson's works

the perimeter fence of the dye works site. As the path makes a left-right zigzag, straight ahead is the site of a dry dock, now infilled. At the end of the dry dock site, the path turns right to head uphill alongside a small stream. This must have been culverted under the canal, and probably the dry dock would have drained into this same culvert. If the canal and overflow here were reinstated and linked to the already watered section just before Bullbridge, it would alleviate flooding problems.

As the path swings to the left, the tree growth along and within the chain link fence shows just how much trees grow in forty years. Where the path comes to a T-junction, turn left on to what was once Hag Lane, linking Chase Road through to Fritchley. After only about 20 yards look out for a path leading off to the right towards a flight of steps. This is your route to Ambergate.

However, if you want to see the route of the canal through Stevenson's from the other end, continue straight on for 200 yards. After a left bend you will see, on the right, part of National Grid's headquarters (formerly Transco) and the path begins to descend. On the left through the trees you can glimpse the reservoir that Stevenson's built on the line of the canal adjacent to the northern portal of Hag Tunnel. (This is easier to see in winter!). Return to the junction of paths and turn left.

The rather daunting flight of steps is not so much the 39 steps as the 93 steps (actually 94!) at the top of which the path swings to the right, then left to reach a small gate in a wall. Pass through then turn left as

The 94 Steps encountered while diverting round the Stevenson and Transco Works

indicated by the way marker to follow the stone wall. This section can be particularly muddy. As the path begins to descend, some power lines appear on the right. At the second pole (a single one) note a short length of brick wall on your left. This is the parapet of the bridge where George Stephenson's 1-in-4 incline on his railway crossed under the path, and the arch of the bridge can still be seen in the undergrowth below. The metre-gauge railway was built to carry

We re-join the canal line by this overflow weir

limestone from Crich to his kilns which were once beside the canal on what is now land belonging to National Grid.

The path continues downhill and back up again, running between the power lines and the chain link fence. As both swing to the left at the second way-marker, so does the path and you descend, continuing between the two, to a stile, beyond which a path takes you back to the canal at an overflow weir. You will be pleased to learn that it is all level from here to Cromford!

There is now water in the channel and a good towpath, which is easily followed through to Cromford, thanks to Derbyshire County Council who own this final 5½ miles. Carry on under a water pipe bridge (another line from the Derwent Valley reservoirs, this time towards Derby) and through Poyser's Bridge No. 16, an intact stone bridge. Note the now fading painted bridge number. We carry on for a short distance to Gratton's Bridge No. 15.

Hay's Wharf in winter

Photo: Hugh Potter

From this bridge all the way to Cromford the canal falls within the Derwent Valley Mills World Heritage Site, and as such is the longest length of canal so designated in England. Just beyond here is the site of Hay's Wharf, with the old stone wharf building nicely restored. A little further on we come to Molds Wharf with its smaller stone cottage, known locally as 'Percy's cottage' after Percy Wilson who lived there till his death in 2009. Note the date 1776 on a stone lintel, meaning it was built before the canal. Beside this on the end of the cottage is a stone chimney which is rather more modern, being dated 1902. Continue along this wooded section for about half a mile to arrive at Chase Bridge No. 14, another intact stone arch, with seats by the towpath on each side. The track which passes over this bridge also crosses a bridge over the railway which is immediately adjacent.

A little further along look out for a concrete milepost on the towpath indicating 3½ miles to Cromford. In this case the original milestone on the opposite side is still intact and is marked Cromford 3½ miles on the one side and Langley 11 miles on the reverse.

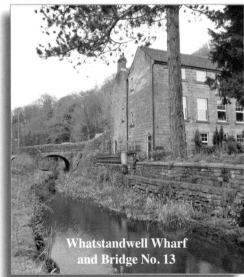

Whatstandwell Wharf and Bridge No. 13

A very pleasant stretch of canal to Whatstandwell follows. Shortly pass a small sewage works on the left as we approach Whatstandwell station. This station is immediately adjacent to the canal, with a fine restored footbridge over the line. There is access from the towpath across this bridge to the station platform. Crich Council Footbridge No. 13a is also here and carries the footpath from the station over the canal and up into Whatstandwell village.

We now approach Whatstandwell Wharf on the right, opposite Eden House, a stone house on the towpath side built over the railway tunnel, just before Whatstandwell Bridge No. 13, another stone arch, with the former wharf house beside it.

The Derwent Hotel, where food is served, is just down the hill alongside the A6. By the towpath just beyond Whatstandwell Bridge is a useful car parking area.

The attractive scenery of the Derwent Valley is now becoming apparent.

An attractive walk through the woods as we approach Robin Hood

Sims Bridge No. 12 follows. This former railway bridge from the gritstone quarries across the canal now has a modern steel footbridge deck on the old stone abutments and still bears traces of the painted bridge number. Shortly pass a water let-off paddle, one of several along this length, complete with wooden railings. Adjacent to this is a narrowing of the

An original bridge Number Plate

canal with stop plank grooves. Following another stone built narrow section, we pass over a culvert which still carries its original No. 10 bridge plate on the towpath wall. This is the only surviving original bridge number plate on the entire canal. Opposite here at Robin Hood, is a former stone sawmill now converted into an attractive house, where bed and breakfast is provided.

A further 100 yards on is a concrete 21/2 mile post on the towpath. Opposite, and somewhat hidden, an original milestone is still in place showing 21/2 miles to Cromford and 12 miles to Langley.

Next is Lea Shaw Bridge No. 9 with worn stone steps adjacent which lead up to an interesting group of old stone farm buildings, some of which are now let out as holiday accommodation.

We then reach Gregory Widehole, which is followed by the

The former Sawmill at Robin Hood

short Gregory Tunnel. Either walk through on the towpath, or if preferred take the path on the left and over the top. The modern concrete 2 mile post is a little further on. After this is a section of stone wall, which marks an overflow carrying excess canal water into the river.

A little further on is another interesting feature, the iron trough aqueduct (Bridge No. 7) which carries the canal over the railway. Notice the portal of Lea Wood railway tunnel adjacent to the aqueduct on the offside. The aqueduct is at present stanked off and drained pending repairs to the corroded ironwork. The towpath is meanwhile carried over on a temporary scaffolding footbridge.

Wigwell Aqueduct and Leawood Pumphouse

Follow the towpath round a right hand bend to a junction with the Leawood or Nightingale Arm, which turns off to the right. If you wish to explore this arm see page 28. At the junction, the towpath crosses from left to right via Swingbridge No. 6. To continue on the main line towards Cromford, pass over the swingbridge and turn left to cross

Wigwell or Leawood Aqueduct. This elegant structure crosses the River Derwent in a single span and is perhaps best seen from below to appreciate the fine lines. To do this, one needs to scramble down the bank to river level. This is best done by taking the path on the opposite side of the canal, on the Cromford side of the aqueduct.

Wigwell Aqueduct from below

Continuing on the towpath over the aqueduct, the 1849 Leawood Pumphouse is on the right between canal and river. This impressive stone building contains a large beam engine which was used to pump water up from the River Derwent to feed the canal. This has been restored to working order and is steamed by enthusiasts on several weekends in the summer. See page 17 for details.

Almost opposite this is the former transhipment warehouse with its canopy over the canal, and the stump of a wharf crane. This was the start of the Cromford and High Peak Railway which was built to connect the Cromford Canal over the Derbyshire hills to the Peak Forest Canal at Whaley Bridge, via a series of steep rope-worked inclines. The line has now been converted into a walking and cycle way.

The enthusiast will no doubt wish to explore this fascinating link separately.

The former transhipment shed at High Peak Junction

Continue along the towpath a short distance to Railway End Swingbridge No. 2. Across this bridge are the High Peak Junction Workshops and the bottom of the Sheep Pasture Incline of the Cromford and High Peak Railway.

Here there are toilets, a useful information centre and a shop selling a wide range of interesting items as well as some refreshments. One can

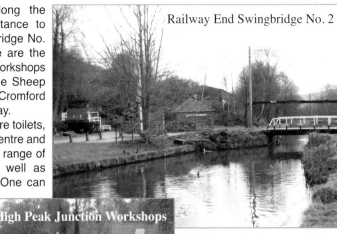

Railway End Swingbridge No. 2

High Peak Junction Workshops

Photo: Hugh Potter

visit the workshops and follow an audio tour for a small charge. This is also the office of the Canal Ranger Service run by Derbyshire County Council.

Re-join the towpath and continue along the pleasant final mile of the canal to pass the stone-arched Lawn Bridge No. 1, and then shortly reach Cromford Wharf.

This is a classic canal terminus in an idyllic setting in the Derwent Valley adjacent to Cromford Meadows. Here the canal widens and divides into two arms with two interesting old stone warehouses, each with a canopy over the canal. The original one on the right, known as the Gothic Warehouse, is now used as a meeting room. The left hand one was built when the feeder arm was made navigable in the 1820s and has been converted into a café.

Arkwright's world famous cotton mill is across the road and in the care of the Arkwright Society (see page 27).

Cromford Wharf is a popular spot with a large pay and display car park and public toilets. Like the canal, this whole area is now part of the Derwent Valley Mills World Heritage Site.

Cromford Wharf during a World Heritage Weekend

Photo: Hugh Potter

Cromford Village

Cromford itself is an interesting and historic place in the Derwent Valley which is perhaps most famous for the fact that Richard Arkwright built the world's first successful water driven cotton mill here in 1771. It is an ideal location for water mills having an abundant water supply. A visit to the Arkwright Society's shops in

The Courtyard at Arkwright's Mill which now incorporates various shops

the mill complex opposite the wharf is highly recommended.

To the right from the wharf is the ancient stone bridge over the River Derwent with ruins of the bridge chapel. Continuing in this direction, we come to Cromford railway station with its delightful original buildings dating from 1849.

To the left from the wharf, and across the other side of the A6, is the centre of the village. Passing through the market place and by Arkwright's Greyhound Inn, we come to the mill pond, and at the opposite end a working waterwheel which originally turned a flour mill. Alongside the pond is the Scarthin Book Shop, a bibliophile's paradise which certainly should not be missed. This establishment has published an excellent Guide to Cromford village. See page 35.

Cromford Station

The Mill Pool in Cromford

Waterwheel at former Flour Mill

The Arkwright Society

Built in 1820, this warehouse, the later of the two, is now converted into a café.

The Derwent Valley has been called the Cradle of the Industrial Revolution, its international significance being recognised by UNESCO in December 2001 when part of the valley, between Matlock Bath and Derby, was inscribed as a World Heritage Site. The essential first step towards a place in world history was taken when Richard Arkwright built the first successful water powered cotton spinning mill at Cromford in 1771. The mill remains a monument to his extraordinary genius. At the same time, he developed Cromford into one of the first industrial villages, including workers' cottages, market place and lock up.

The Arkwright Society, based at Cromford Mill, grew out of the Arkwright Festival which in 1971 commemorated the two hundredth anniversary of Arkwright's arrival. It is a registered charity and an amenity society registered with the Civic Society Initiative.

The Society purchased the Cromford Mill site in 1979 and began the difficult task of restoring this important industrial complex. The work has included a massive decontamination programme, clearing the site of chemicals, which were the legacy of more than fifty years as a colour works, manufacturing colour pigments for paints and dyes.

Visitor facilities at Cromford Mill include shops selling books, gifts, cards, embroidery products and soft furnishings for the home in addition to a wholefood restaurant providing a wide range of delicious hot meals and cakes. The canalside wharf building also houses a wildlife café supplying a range of home made hot snacks and sandwiches in addition to a range of books, bird and bat boxes and other pet and garden items.

Joining the Arkwright Society will help to support the restoration and ongoing maintenance of this internationally significant project. Volunteers are always needed to help with the practical daily tasks as well as to help organise many local projects.

Contact the Society at
Cromford Mill, Mill Lane,
Cromford, Derbyshire
DE4 3RQ
Tel: 01629 823256 email:
info@arkwrightsociety.org.uk

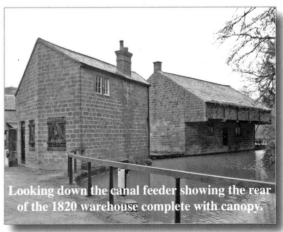

Looking down the canal feeder showing the rear of the 1820 warehouse complete with canopy.

The Leawood or Nightingale Branch

Leawood Junction, where the Leawood Branch leaves to the right

This half mile branch was built in 1802 by Peter Nightingale (great uncle of the famous Florence). The arm used to extend as far as Lea Mills, but following a dispute over water supply, it was truncated and the wharf re-located to the present terminus.

Aqueduct Cottage on the right of the junction has now sadly fallen into disrepair and is almost lost in the foliage.

The main line towpath changes sides here via Swingbridge No. 6. In the background the remains of Aqueduct Cottage are almost lost in the trees.

Aqueduct Cottage around 1900

Photo: FCC Archive

The start of the branch here at Leawood Junction is marked by a stone built narrows, the recesses for the stop gates being clearly visible. There was a wooden footbridge over the narrows giving access to the cottage, but this has been replaced by a concrete stank. From here walk along the left bank of the branch.

28

At first the towpath traverses a narrow strip of land between the River Derwent and the canal. The channel, which is sometimes in water, soon ends abruptly at the site of an iron trough aqueduct over the railway. This is in a very similar situation to the railway aqueduct on the main line of the canal described in the Third Stage section, being at the opposite end of Lea Wood railway tunnel. In this case the aqueduct has

Site of Aqueduct over Railway

disappeared and has been replaced by a steel footbridge to carry the towpath over the railway.

Beyond here the canal bed is dry but intact. The towpath makes a pleasant walk through Lea Wood to the wharf at the terminus. Just before the wharf, there is a small stone building on the towpath. Note that this incorporates a stone gatepost with the familiar grooves worn by horseboat towlines. There would have been a gate across the towpath here to keep the wharf secure. The wharfinger's stone cottage is intact and has been extended to make an attractive private residence. On the edge of the wharf, the remains of a

Leawood Wharf and Wharf House

wooden crane stump with an iron turntable can still be discerned.

The branch terminates shortly beyond this wharf. From this point retrace your steps to rejoin the main line. Alternatively, continue on the public footpath which turns left here, to join the road in Lea Bridge.

Base of crane on Leawood Wharf

The Pinxton Branch
Ironville to Pinxton - 2¹/4 miles

Top Lock Bridge No. 1

The Pinxton Branch leaves the main line of the Cromford Canal at Ironville, adjacent to the site of Top of Flight Lock No. 1. This 2¹/4 mile branch ran on one level from Ironville through Pye Bridge to Pinxton Wharf.

As mentioned earlier in this guide, the top lock was removed in the 1980s and the level of Codnor Park Reservoir lowered as part of an ill-conceived flood relief scheme. This means that Top Lock Bridge No. 1, a fine intact stone arch over the entrance to the branch, now stands in isolation.

The towpath at the start of the branch was on the right through this bridge but this is very overgrown. The better path now begins on the left hand side, passing along the eastern end of Codnor Park Reservoir, on top of the retaining wall. This separates the reservoir on the left from the now infilled Pinxton Branch on the right.

On reaching the north east corner of the reservoir, the Pinxton Branch turns to the right and passes under Butterley Company Bridge No. 2 which nowadays has a modern steel footbridge deck on the old abutments.

The canal line in Ironville with Church Bridge No. 3 in the distance

The path now lies in the infilled canal bed, and continues with an old stone towpath wall on the right. A vehicle access joins the canal line and leads to the back of Ironville Church Hall, where there is a car park on the former canal bed. A board here tells us we are now on the Derbyshire County Council Pinxton Canal Path. We then pass through a motor cycle barrier and continue close to the rear of Ironville Church and vicarage with the cemetery on the left, and under Ironville or Church Bridge No. 3. This was originally a stone arch bridge but is now a modern flat-decked structure, strengthened underneath with a concrete buttress. See inside back cover.

Railway Bridge No. 4

Photo: Hugh Potter

Beyond here the infilled canal line is grassed over and swings to the left, passing the last of the houses in Ironville including a fine stone house on the left, which was formerly the vicarage, and then under Railway Bridge No. 4. This is the former Midland Railway's Ambergate & Pye Bridge Branch which has been taken over by the Midland Railway Centre. Steam trains can quite often be seen on this bridge.

More details of the Midland Railway Centre's activities are given on page 34.

The good path continues after the railway bridge on the right hand side of the infilled canal. About 200 yards further on, a road crosses the canal line at a low level between stone walls. This is the site of Fletchers Row Bridge No. 5, which carried Nottingham Lane. There is a modern concrete 1/2 mile post still in situ just beyond here.

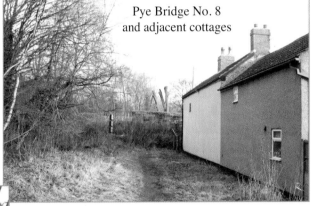

Pye Bridge No. 8 and adjacent cottages

PINXTON CANAL PATH

DERBYSHIRE
County Council
Countryside Service

IRONVILLE
CAR PARK

For Information
Tel. 01629 580000

The next section is a pleasant walk along a landscaped stretch where a large number of small trees have been planted. The path passes through the centre of these, but there is no sign of the canal. Shortly a footpath crosses the line. This is the site of Oakes Tramway Bridge No. 6 and Red Bridge No. 7, which were adjacent to each other, but have now both disappeared. The tree lined section continues, and after passing a sewage works on the right, we approach Pye Bridge pond on the left. This is all that now remains of Pye Bridge basin and wharf.

We then continue to Main Road Bridge No. 8 at Pye Bridge. This bridge is infilled but intact, now with a flat deck and steel railings. The old canalside cottages survive by the bridge.

31

Cross over the road and down the steps to continue along the towpath which is on the right of the infilled canal, with some of the stone towpath wall remaining. The Dog & Doublet public house, which is a short distance down the road from the bridge, may also be reached from the towpath at this point.

The path again passes through a great many young trees planted on the landscaped canal. As with many infilled canals, drainage is a problem here and the path can be very muddy in wet weather.

We shortly come to Railway Bridge No. 9. This is a twin-arched blue brick structure which carries the main Erewash Valley railway over the canal line.

Immediately after this bridge we encounter the former Smotherfly opencast coal site, a major obstacle to the canal. This area has been opencast mined, which has greatly altered the lie of the land. The River Erewash was diverted and the canal line completely obliterated. When the extraction of coal was completed, the River Erewash was returned to its original course. This has left the diversion channel, which is approximately on the original canal line and can be seen through this railway bridge, dry and isolated. The Friends of the Cromford Canal are making plans to use this channel as part of the restoration of the canal, but in the meantime, to carry on with the walk to Pinxton we must follow an extensive diversion for about a mile.

Do not pass under the railway bridge, but turn sharp left on to a footpath

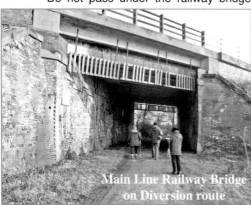

Main Line Railway Bridge on Diversion route

immediately before it. Follow this path, alongside a metal fence as it crosses the remains of a former railway embankment, and then continue on the path with the main line railway on your right. The path is fenced off from the adjacent fields on the left. After approx. 1/2 mile pass over 2 stiles, turn right onto a track and walk under the main line railway.

Follow this track straight ahead for some 500 yards and through a branch railway bridge. Just beyond this bridge we can again see the opencast area and the dry channel where the River Erewash had been diverted.

Turn immediately left to cross a small wooden bridge over a stream and follow the footpath. This runs closely along the right hand side of the railway for another 500 yards, then turns sharp right, away from the railway and alongside a commercial vehicle scrapyard for a short distance.

We emerge through a dismantled stile and turn right, away from the scrapyard gates along a track. We then pass the site of Colliery Office Bridge No. 11, and Railway Bridge No. 12, both of which are long gone. The track passes through two gates and we then arrive beside some recognisable canal!

The channel is in water here which runs over a weir at this

Site of Palmerston Swingbridge No. 13

Approaching Pinxton

end. The towpath has been widened into a track which is the access road to the scrapyard. This has meant that the canal is narrower than originally built, but it is full of water!

After a steel barrier the track then leaves to the right, and the towpath continues ahead alongside the water and through a motorcycle barrier. There is a low level footbridge across the canal which has been built on the original stone abutments of Palmerston Swingbridge No. 13.

We then shortly come to a small canalside terrace followed by the Boat Inn. This is an old canal pub which has been enlarged and modernised. There is then another low level footbridge across the canal. One can cross this bridge and take a path round the terminal basin at Pinxton. This former wharf is a large area of water which has been restored

by Derbyshire County Council and Broxtowe District Council. It provides a pleasant landscaped area with seats etc. and is also a thriving fishery. The railway is adjacent and we cross over the level crossing to give access to the village and buses if required. The main road through Pinxton is called Wharf Road, which is perhaps indicative of the importance of the canal in times past.

Pinxton Basin and Wharf

The Midland Railway - Butterley

by Alan Calladine

Crossing the
Butterley Reservoir

Robin Stewart-Smith

The route of the Midland . Railway-Butterley line parallels the Cromford Canal from Ironville through to the western end of Butterley tunnel where it too is blocked by the A38. The original Midland Railway Company bought out the Cromford Canal and following this tradition the Railway Museum now also owns a short length of canal from the Newlands Inn to the Butterley Tunnel eastern portal.

Walking up the canal from Ironville you will see the railway line higher up the valley on the right hand side and may see some passing trains. By climbing the steps in the cutting just beyond the Newlands Inn you first come across the terminus station of the Golden Valley Light Railway on which narrow gauge trains run on most weekends between April and October and daily during many of the school holidays. This line uses a range of equipment and vehicles acquired from varied industrial sources, mainly local collieries. If trains are running you can use the line to take you to the Railway Museum site at Swanwick Junction or you can continue walking around the end of the line and climb further up the bank through the Midland Railway-Butterley Country Park. The path then continues through the Country Park with the narrow gauge railway on the left and the standard gauge railway on the right. This 35 acre Country Park was acquired by the railway and the paths and ponds that you can see have been created to make a very pleasant area. A stile at the end of the Country Park leads to a public footpath which crosses both railways. You can then turn left up the footpath a short distance and take the right fork leading to the railway's Swanwick Junction site. This site contains a large Railway Museum, The Princess Royal Class Locomotive Trust Depot, The Midland Diesel Group Collection, the headquarters of the Golden Valley Light Railway and much more including a Demonstration Signal Box, a Victorian Railwayman's Church, and Brittain Pit Farm Park. All this is well worth exploring.

If the standard gauge railway is running there is the option to travel on this through Butterley station and across Butterley Reservoir to Hammersmith at the western end of Butterley Tunnel. See page 11.

The Midland Railway-Butterley is one of the leading railway preservation sites in the country with its impressive range of locomotives and rolling stock together with other railway infrastructure such as signal boxes and stations, all of which have been built since the railway was taken over in the early 1970s. Virtually everything that you see has been moved from various parts of the country to the railway to bring back its former glory.

Further information is available from Midland Railway-Butterley,
Butterley Station, Ripley, Derbyshire DE5 3QZ, by telephone on 01773 570140
or by visiting the web site at www.midlandrailwaycentre.co.uk.

Further Reading

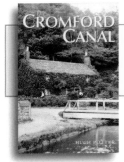

The Cromford Canal by Hugh Potter £12.99 plus £2.20 p&p
This 128 page softback book contains many rare and historical photographs of our canal, with extended captions giving much well researched information.

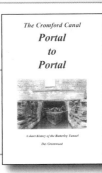

Portal to Portal by Des Greenwood £6.50 plus £1.85 p&p
A short history of the Butterley Tunnel.
This 49 page softback book contains rare photographs of the tunnel interior and the unique loading wharf from the Butterley Works giving access to boats waiting below.

There and Back Again by Simon Stoker £14.99 plus £2.20 p&p
This 128 page softback book relates the restoration work carried out by the Cromford Canal Society on the upper part of the Cromford Canal from 1968 to 1988.

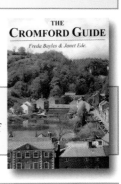

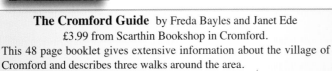

The Cromford Guide by Freda Bayles and Janet Ede
£3.99 from Scarthin Bookshop in Cromford.
This 48 page booklet gives extensive information about the village of Cromford and describes three walks around the area.

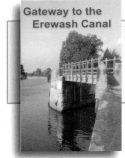

Gateway to the Erewash Canal £3.50 plus 95p. p&p
Published by the
Erewash Canal Preservation & Development Association.
This 20 page booklet describes the history of the Erewash Canal, the restoration and present day features from Trent Lock to Langley Mill.

All items except where stated are available from
Friends of the Cromford Canal Sales.
Visit our website: www.cromfordcanal.org.uk

Return Transport

By Bus:

There is a generally good bus service in this area and this is probably the most convenient option. Return transport is possible by bus at least once an hour for either the whole canal or any of the sections described in this guide. For up to date details of the routes and journey times to suit your requirements, telephone the East Midlands Traveline number: **0871 200 2233**

Alternatively, visit **www.travelineeastmidlands.co.uk** where your best option can be selected and a timetable downloaded if preferred.

By Train:

Langley Mill station is about 10 minutes walk from the canal on the main A608 road through Langley Mill.

There are no rail services at Ironville, Pinxton or Bullbridge.

Ambergate station is near the junction of the A610 with the A6. To reach the canal, walk north on the A6 for 200 yards, turn right up Chase Road and pass under the railway to join the canal at Poyser's Bridge No.16.

Whatstandwell station is close by the canal alongside the A6. There is direct access from the station to the towpath via the footbridge.

Cromford station is reached from the wharf by turning right from the wharf entrance and over the river bridge. Keep right after the bridge and follow the road for 300 yards. The station is up a road to the left.

The three last have car parking facilities.

Cromford to Langley Mill or vice versa takes about 1 hr 45 mins, changing at Nottingham. Cromford to Whatstandwell or Ambergate takes only a few minutes. In all cases there is an hourly service.

Again, since timetables change regularly, it is best to obtain up to date information by either telephoning the national rail enquiry number: **08457 484950** or visit **www.eastmidlandstrains.co.uk** to check on the best options.

By Car:

In addition to the station car parks above, convenient car parking places near the canal are as follows:-

Langley Mill	Linkmel Road near the Great Northern Basin.
Ironville	Car park on the canal line near Codnor Park Reservoir. (Page 8)
Pinxton	On the approach to the Boat Inn beyond the Basin.
Lower Hartshay	At the closed end of the former main Ripley road by the Gate Inn.
Bullbridge	On the street by the Canal Inn.
Whatstandwell	Small car park on the canal side by Whatstandwell Bridge No. 13.
High Peak Junction	Car park across the railway and river from the canal on Lea Road.
Cromford	Large car park at the Wharf (Pay and Display) or on the adjacent Cromford Meadows.